Space Explorers
EARTH

First Published in Great Britain in 2020 by Buttercup Publishing Ltd.
46 Syon Lane, Isleworth, Greater London, TW7 5NQ, UK

Copyright © Buttercup Publishing Ltd. 2020
All rights reserved. No part of this book may be reproduced or transmitted in any form or by any electronic or mechanical means, including information storage and retrieval systems, without permission in writing from the publisher.

Author: Andrea Kaczmarek
Illustrator: Alexandra Colombo
Series Editor: Kirsty Taylor

A Cataloguing-in-Publishing record for this book is available from the British Library.

ISBN: 978-1-912422-89-0

www.buttercuppublishing.co.uk
contact@buttercuppublishing.co.uk
Printed and bound in China

Twins, Daisy and Dan, were *very* excited. They were visiting Grandpa today! They loved Grandpa, but what they *really* wanted to see was his brand-new telescope.

The telescope sat at the very top of the house,
up the winding stairs, by the biggest window. They heard that it
was HUGE and could transport them to outer space by just looking through it!
They couldn't wait to explore!

"Grandpa! Grandpa!" Dan squealed. "Can we go the moon? Or zoom through the stars? Or bounce across a planet if we look through the telescope?"

Grandpa laughed. "We can try! But not right now, it's too bright. We will have to wait until night-time."

Daisy and Dan couldn't wait. "Hurry up night-time! We want to explore!"

Daisy and Dan watched as Grandpa picked up a big blue and green ball and spun it on his finger. "Before we become science explorers, I have a question!"

"Where are we now?" he asked.

The twins giggled, "In your house, Grandpa!"

Grandpa chuckled, "Well, yes. But we live on planet Earth."
"All explorers need to know about Earth before they set off into space!" he said, with a smile on his face.

"Tell us, Grandpa! Tell us please!" the twins begged.

"Daisy, you can be the sun." He gave her a large orange and placed it on her head.

"The Earth travels around it. Stand in the middle."
"I'm daytime?" Daisy asked, as she moved to the middle of the room, trying not to lose the orange resting delicately on her head.
"That's right!" said Grandpa.

"Dan, you can be the moon. Here, take this."
Dan placed a banana on his head and started to run around the room.

"Slow down, moon! You travel around the Earth, so stay close to me," Grandpa exclaimed. "You are night-time."

"When the Earth is near Daisy, I mean, the Sun, it is warmer. So, when it is further away from the Sun, it is colder." Grandpa slowly walked around Daisy, trying to avoid tripping over Dan as he was still a little over-excited!

"Because I, or the Earth, tilts, the places closer to the Sun will feel warmer, and the places further away will feel colder. That is how we have seasons."

"Earth spins and tilts as it moves around the Sun so that everyone experiences the seasons. It's a very busy planet!"

Dan started to peel the banana. Daisy looked at him and shook her head, trying not to laugh. "Does that mean that it is winter on the other side of the Earth when it is summer here?"

Grandpa stopped spinning as he was feeling a little dizzy. "That's right, Daisy."

"The Earth follows a path around the Sun and the Moon moves around the Earth. That is how we get day and night, summer and winter."

**December 22
Winter Solstice**

"That's pretty cool, Grandpa. Do we know enough to be science explorers now?" Dan asked, having eaten all of his banana and staring longingly at Daisy's orange.

"Get ready for bed and we shall see." Grandpa answered, taking the orange before Dan could grab it.

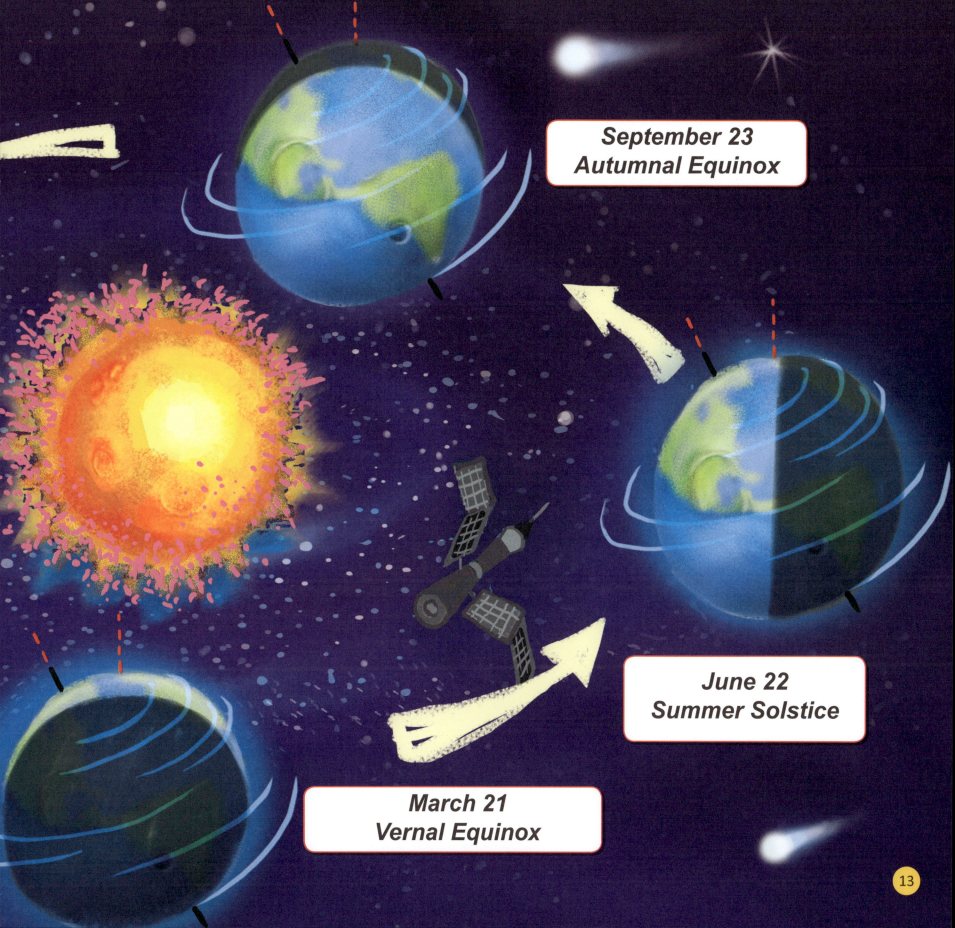

The twins couldn't wait. They brushed their teeth, like all good science explorers do, and raced back up the winding stairs to the top of the house.

Grandpa had promised that something extra special would be waiting for them. He also told them that they would need to bring science explorer snacks. It was going to be a long night after all.

"It's a spaceship!" Dan shouted. His smile was so wide, he was certain it could be seen on the other side of planet Earth.

There, in the corner of the telescope room, sat a big box with wings. It even had stars and lights hanging above it!

"Science explorers need a lot of strength, so have a little nap and I'll wake you both when the stars start to shine." Grandpa promised.

COSMODAI......

"But Grandpa," Daisy cried, "how can we sleep when our spaceship doesn't have a name!"

Grandpa scratched his chin, "How about cosmos? It's the word used to describe where all of the planets, stars and moons are."

Daisy thought hard, squinting through her glasses. "Could the spaceship have our names on it too?"

"COSMODAISYDAN! The bestest, fastest, coolest spaceship that ever was!" shouted Dan.

Grandpa smiled as Daisy scribbled the name onto the box-like ship.

After all that excitement, the twins fell fast asleep in COSMODAISYDAN as Grandpa watched out for the twinkling stars.

The sky grew dark and the stars appeared. The moon shone pale and bright. Grandpa gently woke the sleeping science explorers, just as he had promised.

"Time for COSMODAISYDAN's first trip to the moon," he whispered softly. "Take a look through the telescope and you might see it. It is a little cloudy tonight."

"Is it turning?" Daisy yawned, rubbing her eyes. "It is always turning, and so are we …"

The children took it turns to look through the big, red telescope. Their very first mission was almost complete.

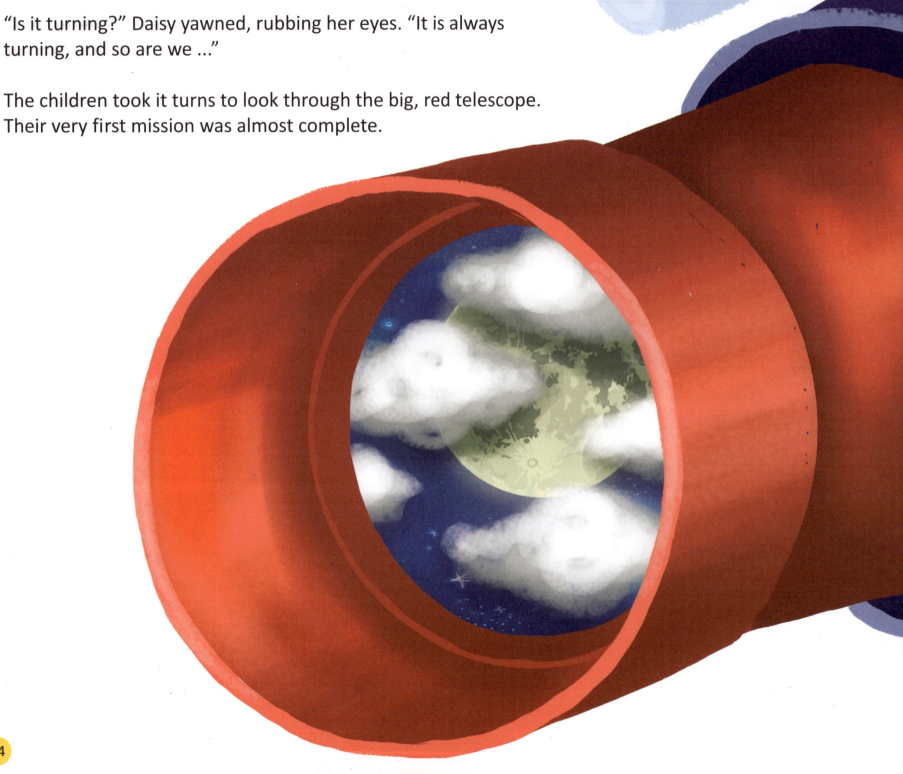

After a while, the twins grew tired. "Time to fly back to planet Earth."

Grandpa scooped them up in his big, strong arms and tucked them back up into COSMODAISYDAN.

He smiled at the sleepy twins as they groaned. "We will see the moon and the stars another time, when the clouds are gone," Grandpa promised.

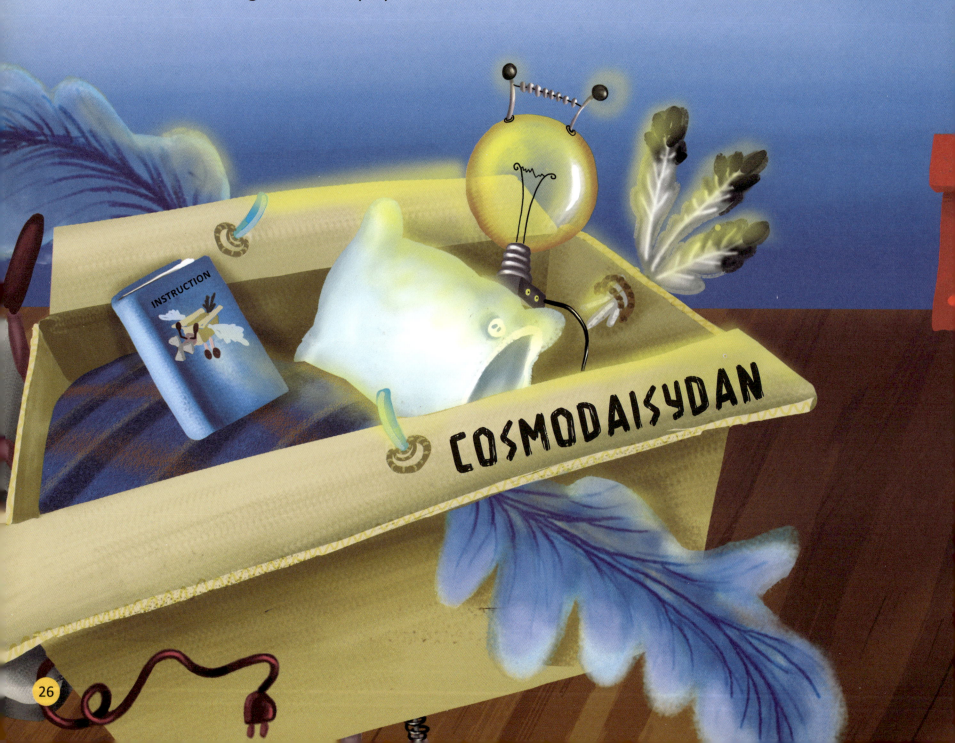

The science explorers yawned. They could barely keep their eyes open. They couldn't wait for their next big science adventure.

The Earth turns around each day and the moon circles around the Earth. At night, we can see the moon and in daytime we see the bright sun.

Earth

Moon

The Sun is the very centre of our Solar System. It shines bright and gives us daylight. But never look directly at the sun, its strong brightness can hurt our eyes.

Sun

With a telescope you can see things that are far away, much clearer, and they look nearer. A telescope magnifies things – it makes things look much bigger – it has special glass lenses to do this.

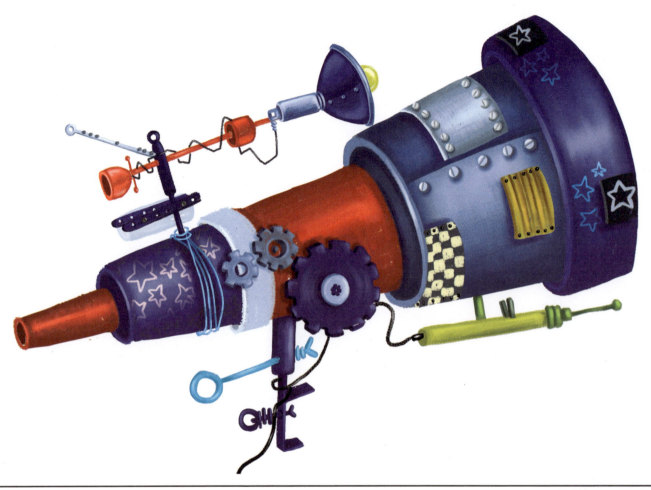

"In the infinite sky, there is a bright star, I love you Kay to the moon and back"

with love
Alexandra Colombo